MUNCHIE BOOKS

This book belongs to

_____

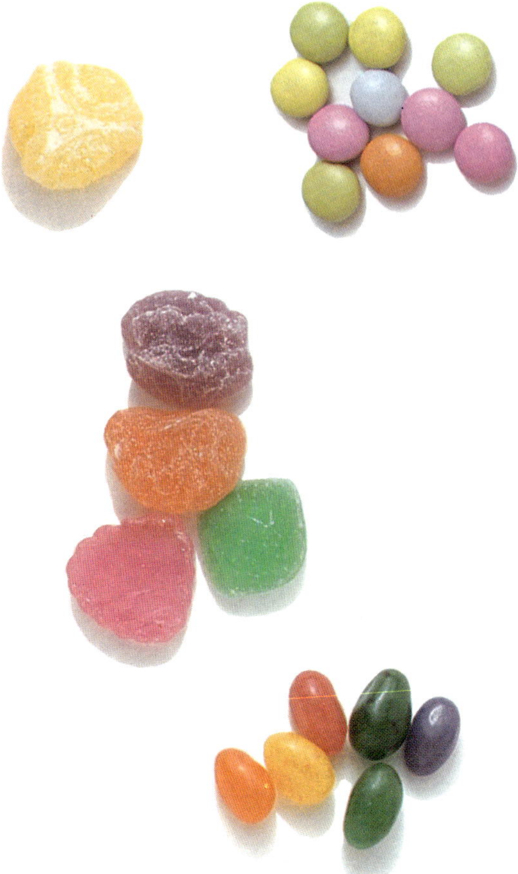

CANDIES & GOODIES

CONTENTS

Introduction 5
Recipes 7
Cold-Water Test 62

Designed, Produced, and Published by
Allen D. Bragdon Publishers, Inc.
153 West 82nd Street
New York, NY 10024

Copyright by Allen D. Bragdon Publishers, Inc. No
part of this book may be reproduced or utilized for profit in any
form or by any means whatever, including electronic or mechanical copying, recording, storage and retrieval of text, data, or images
by any system without permission in writing from the publisher.

Many of these recipes were developed by Marion Ham and originally published in Gifts From a Country Kitchen; illustrations by
Carolyn Ringland.
ISBN 0-916410-14-5   Printed in Hong Kong

INTRODUCTION

Homemade candies are interesting to prepare and pure magic in the way a few simple ingredients are transformed into professional-looking delicacies. Only the best commercial candies can duplicate the authentic richness and flavor of homemade creations made with real butter, cream, fruits, and nuts. Home-salted and candied nuts, too, are so very different from commercial snack foods that they will become prized gifts.

For all their beauty, candies are relatively simple to make. For best results use a candy thermometer to gauge temperature accurately. You can also use the cold-water test described at the end of the book, but it is not as precise. If your thermometer's been jangling around in a kitchen drawer for a year or two, it's probably best to test it before making a batch of candy. Immerse it in a pan of water and gradually bring the water to a boil. Allow it to boil for 10 minutes—temperature should read 212°F at sea level, and one degree less for every 500 feet in altitude.

Before plunging your thermometer in hot syrup, warm it gradually.

One time-honored caution: candy is best made in dry weather. So if the humidity is high, heat the syrup two degrees higher than called for to compensate for increased moisture in the air.

Candies should be cooked in heavy saucepans of the capacity called for in each recipe. Thick metal distributes heat from the flame or coil so the syrup is less likely to burn on the hot-spot. The liquid will expand as it boils and bubble up to two or three times its original volume when cold. Use a long-handled wooden spoon because the liquid is likely to spatter.

A clean pastry brush and a cup of cold water also come in handy to wash sugar crystals off the sides of the pan. Crystals, while not the end of the world, are a problem to the home candy-maker. To prevent them from forming in candy, dissolve sugar in liquid before heating. As the mixture cooks, stir slowly and in one direction only, being careful not to pick up crystals as they form on the sides of the pan.

Candy making is a science—changing a liquid (sugar syrup) into a solid—so be sure to follow heating, working, and shaping instructions carefully. With the recipes here, and attention to the details of making candies, your holiday creations can be cheerfully impressive, and will give you a well-earned sense of accomplishment.

Peanut Butter Buckeyes

  1¾ cups peanut butter
  1 cup butter or margarine, softened
  4¼ cups confectioners sugar
  2 cups semisweet chocolate pieces
  1 tablespoon vegetable oil
  Toothpicks

In large bowl cream together peanut butter and butter or margarine until light and creamy. Add sugar and mix well. Roll into small balls about ¾-inch in diameter. Place on waxed paper and chill for 8 hours or overnight. Melt chocolate pieces and oil in top of double boiler over hot, not boiling, water until completely melted. Using toothpicks spear each ball, dip lower half into melted chocolate, and return to waxed paper. Refrigerate to harden. Store between layers of waxed paper in airtight containers. Keep in a cool place.

To make Cherry Chocolate Morsels, follow procedure for making peanut butter cream. Instead of rolling into balls, wrap it around stemmed maraschino cherries. Proceed as for Buckeyes, rolling candies in finely ground pistachio nuts after dipping in chocolate. Refrigerate to harden.

Gift Idea:

These chocolate tasties look pretty wrapped three to a square of colored cellophane. Or fit several Buckeyes snugly into a deep yellow cereal bowl or saucer so the Buckeye shows its tawny heart. Overwrap in plastic film and tie the package with green yarn.

9

Salted Oven Pecans

 1 pound (4 cups) pecan halves
 ¼ pound butter
   Salt

In large heavy skillet bake nuts with butter at 250°F for 1 hour, stirring occasionally. Cool and sprinkle with salt. Store in a covered container.

Gift Idea:

Fill a small crock or coffee mug with nuts. Seal with plastic wrap and tie a ribbon around the handle. An inexpensive cereal bowl also makes a fine container. Wrap in plastic film and the nuts are ready to serve when you hand this gift to your host or hostess.

Christmas Party Walnut Crunchies

Makes 2 cups
Preparation time: 30 minutes
Baking time: 50 minutes

- 2 cups walnuts, coarsely chopped
- 4 tablespoons butter
- 1 egg white
- ½ cup sugar
- ⅛ teaspoon salt
- ¼ teaspoon cinnamon

Serve these as after dinner nuts. The subtle sweet spicy flavor complements any meal. Preheat oven to 300°F. Spread nuts over bottom of 13 x 9-inch baking dish. Dot with 2 tablespoons butter. Bake 20 minutes, stirring frequently. Add remaining 2 tablespoons butter and mix well. Beat egg white stiff; add sugar, salt, and cinnamon and beat well. Stir into nuts, mix well. Bake at 325°F for 30 minutes. Cool. Break into pieces. Store in covered container.

Gift Idea:

Plastic sandwich bags filled with Walnut Crunchies and decorated with a Christmas seal and ribbon make a thoughtful gift from your country kitchen. Or pack in a gift highball glass—the perfect holder for these walnuts. Pack the walnuts loosely; cover with plastic wrap and your gift is ready to serve the moment you present it

Spiced Nuts

1 pound (4 cups) walnut or pecan halves (or mixed)
1 cup butter
3 cups confectioners sugar
2 tablespoons nutmeg
2 tablespoons cloves
2 tablespoons cinnamon

In heavy skillet toast nuts and butter over low heat for 20 minutes, stirring frequently until lightly browned. Mix together the remaining ingredients in a paper bag. Remove nuts from pan and drain on paper towels. Toss nuts with other ingredients in paper bag until generously coated. Turn into a sieve or colander to shake off excess coating. Cool and store in a covered container.

Gift Idea:

Pile these nuts into a small wooden box (available from craft supply stores); then tie a deep rust-colored ribbon around the box and tuck in a few green sprigs.

Poppycock

- 1½ cups sugar
- ½ cup light corn syrup
- ½ cup water
- ½ teaspoon salt
- 8 cups popped popcorn
- 1 cup toasted almonds, pecans, or peanuts
- 2 tablespoons butter
- 1 teaspoon vanilla extract

Combine sugar, corn syrup, water, and salt. Cook over low heat, stirring constantly, until sugar dissolves. Cook over medium heat to hard-crack stage (300°F), or until small amount dropped into cold water forms hard threads. Meanwhile, spread popcorn and nuts into a buttered jelly-roll pan and heat in oven at 350°F for 10 minutes. Remove syrup from heat and quickly stir in butter and vanilla extract until butter melts. Pour over popcorn mixture. Stir to coat well. Spread in thin layer on a flat surface. Cool and separate into cluster. Makes 2 quarts.

17

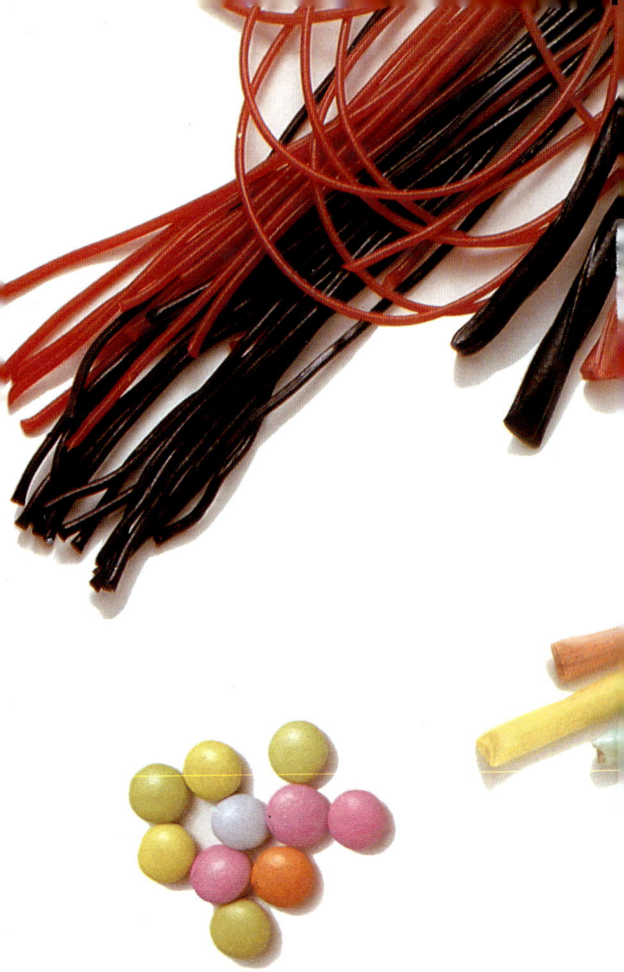

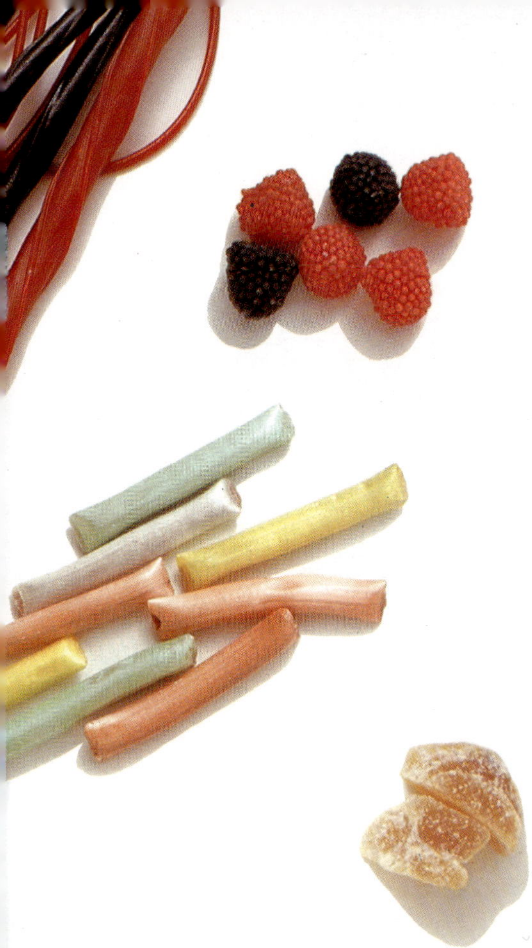

Chocolate Creams

Gift Idea:

These candies are perfect for a "sampler." Place in individual paper candy cups and pack into a gift-wrap covered box. Tie a silk rose on top for a Valentine's Day present. Be sure to keep candy refrigerated until giving.

4¼ cups confectioners sugar
1 cup butter or margarine, softened
2 cups semisweet chocolate pieces
1 tablespoon vegetable oil
Toothpicks
¾ cup crème de menthe, creme de cacao, or 3 tablespoons coconut extract or liqueur
½ cup finely ground nuts or ¾ cup sweetened shredded coconut
Pecans or walnuts, finely chopped for garnish
Shredded coconut for garnish

Cream together butter or margarine and sugar. Add flavorings and nuts or coconut. Proceed as for Peanut Butter Buckeyes. Roll in finely chopped nuts or shredded coconut after dipping in chocolate. Refrigerate to harden.

Old-English Nut Toffee

1 lb. (2 cups) butter
4 cups sifted sugar
2 cups finely chopped nuts
1 lb. milk chocolate
Butter

In a heavy, 3-qt. saucepan, melt butter; add sugar and 1 cup nuts. Place over medium heat and bring to a boil, stirring constantly, until mixture reaches 212°F on a candy thermometer. Then, without stirring, continue to cook over low heat until thermometer reads 300°F. If butter separates or candy browns too rapidly on the sides, do stir briefly. When mixture reaches 300°F, stir gently for a few seconds, then pour at once onto a cool, buttered marble slab or on several buttered cookie sheets. Spread out until candy is ⅛ to ¼ inch thick. Allow to stand a few minutes, then loosen bottom. Melt milk chocolate in top half of a double boiler. When toffee is cold, break up. Cover with melted milk chocolate and remaining nuts. Be sure chocolate has hardened before storing. Toffee will keep several weeks in an airtight tin.

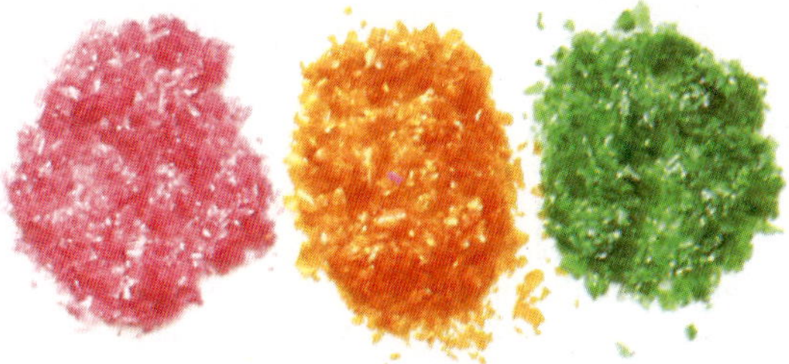

Molasses Taffy for Pulling

- 1 cup sugar
- ½ cup dark brown sugar, firmly packed
- 2 cups dark molasses
- ¾ cup water
- 2 teaspoons white vinegar
- ⅛ teaspoon baking soda
- ¼ teaspoon salt
- Butter
- Oil of peppermint, spearmint, or cinnamon (optional)

Gift Idea:

If you make more than one batch, color code each flavor by wrapping in a different color cellophane. Or tie small pieces of yarn to ends of wrapped candies: green for peppermint, blue for molasses, red for cinnamon, yellow for spearmint, etc. After wrapping fill salvaged glass jars with taffy; screw on the caps and decorate with gummed gift-wrap tape in bright colors.

Gift Idea:

Make small packets of nuts, using colorful nylon net, and tie with contrasting ribbon. Tie on a honey dipper, pie dough cutter, or salt/nut spoon and hang on your tree for a visiting friend.

Chocolate-Nut Squares

  2 squares unsweetened chocolate
½ cup (¼ lb.) butter
  1 cup sugar
½ teaspoon salt
  1 teaspoon vanilla extract
  2 eggs
½ cup sifted flour
½ cup chopped nuts

In top half of a double boiler, melt chocolate and butter together. Add successively: sugar, salt, vanilla, eggs (one at a time), and flour. Mix well. Pour batter into greased shallow baking pan (approximately 15 x 10 inches). Pat nuts firmly on top. Bake at 425°F for 15 minutes; cut while still warm.

Date Loaf-Candy

- 2 cups sugar
- 1 cup milk
- 1 tablespoon butter
- 1 teaspoon vanilla extract
- ½ lb. chopped dates
- 2 cups chopped pecans

Boil sugar, milk, and butter until syrup forms a soft ball when dropped into cold water. Add dates and cook until tender (5 to 10 minutes). Remove from heat; add vanilla extract and pecans. Beat until stiff. Pour onto a damp cloth and shape into a roll. Chill. Wrap in foil and refrigerate until ready to slice. You can refrigerate this for months, but do not freeze.

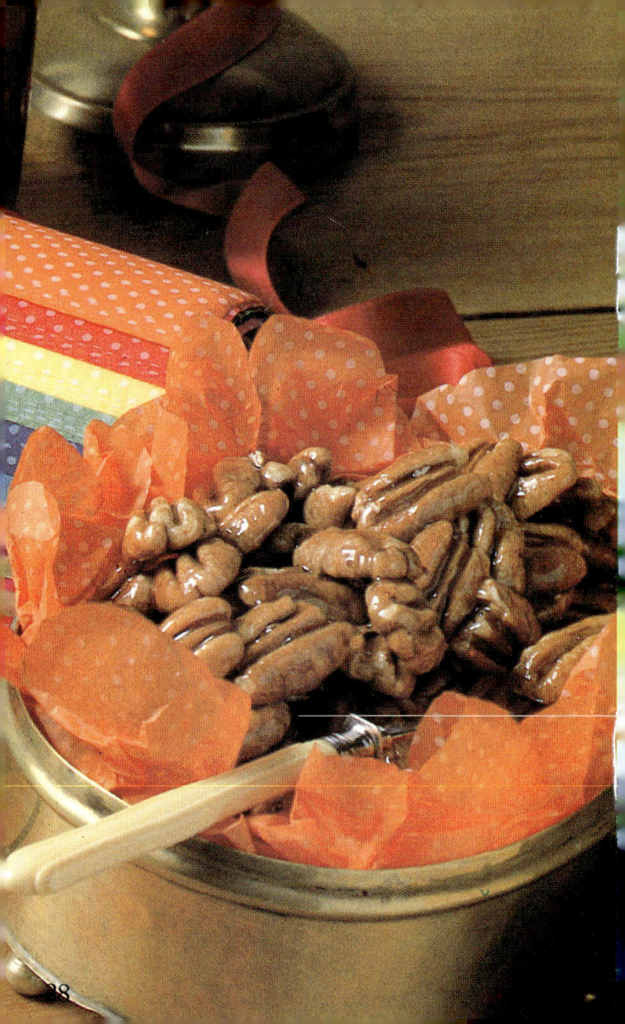

Spiced Pecans

    1 cup sugar
    ½ cup water
    ¼ teaspoon cream of tartar
    ¼ teaspoon cloves
    ½ teaspoon cinnamon
    ½ teaspoon nutmeg
    ½ teaspoon salt
    2 cups pecans

Boil sugar, water and spices to the soft-ball stage, that is, until the syrup forms a soft ball when dropped into cold water. Add pecans. Turn out on buttered, waxed paper and separate nuts so they don't remain in clusters. Let cool.

Southern Penuche

- 2 cups sugar
- 2 cups light brown sugar, firmly packed
- 2 cups light cream
- 1 teaspoon soft butter
- ¾ teaspoon vanilla
- ½ cup walnuts, chopped (optional)

Combine sugars and cream in a 2-quart saucepan, stirring until sugars are dissolved. Boil uncovered without stirring until syrup reaches soft-ball stage (235°F to 240°F). Cool for 10 minutes. Spread out on flat baking dish and beat with a wooden spoon until mixture becomes thick and holds its shape. Add vanilla and nuts. Pour into flat dish, cool thoroughly, and cut into squares. Store in a covered container.

Gift Idea:

For gift giving, stack penuche on an inexpensive crystal dish or plate. Cover with light-colored cellophane and top with a ribbon bow. Penuche squares can also be wrapped individually and packed in a decorative box, the candy cushioned with shredded green paper.

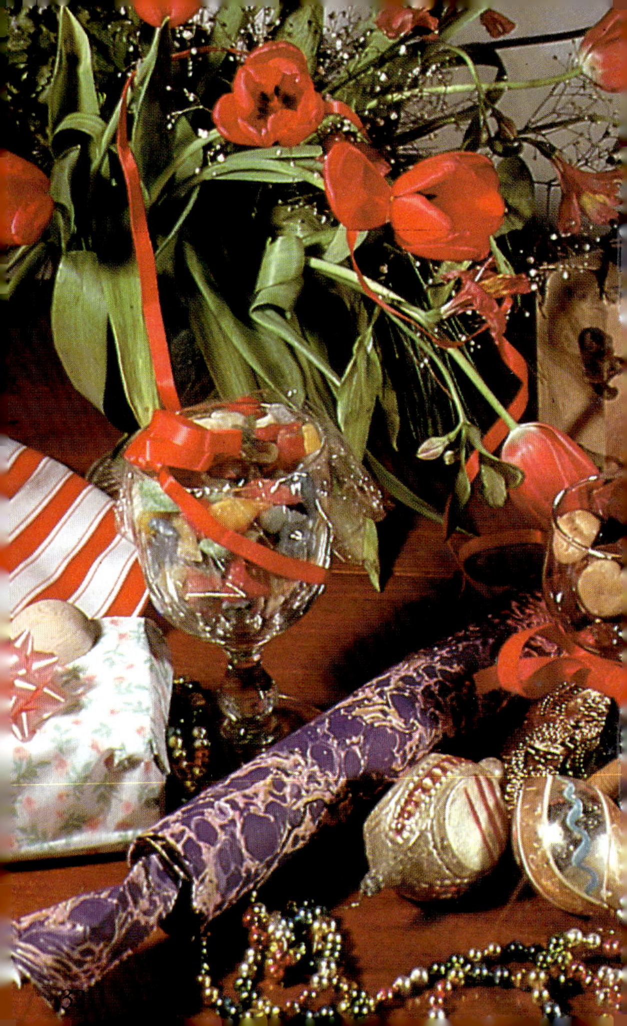

33

Orange Poppy Seed Candies

　¾ cup sugar
　3 cups honey
1½ pounds poppy seeds
　1 cup candied orange peel, diced
　2 cups walnuts, finely chopped
　　Confectioners sugar

In 2-quart saucepan cook honey and sugar over moderate heat until sugar dissolves. Add poppy seeds and boil until mixture reaches hard-crack stage (300°F), about 30 minutes. Add orange peel and nuts and stir until mixture boils. Turn out onto a large platter that has been moistened with cold water. Flatten with a spatula dipped in hot water. Sprinkle with confectioners sugar. Allow to cool 8 to 10 minutes. Cut into small squares.

Gift Idea:

This is a pretty candy and makes a nice gift packed into a glass or plastic goblet. Cover with plastic film and tie a pretty ribbon around stem of goblet.

Fruit and Nut Divinity

Gift Idea:

The fruits and nuts in a snowy white base make a most festive looking Christmas candy. Place in small covered apothecary jars for giving or arrange on a dish and cover with plastic film. For a party, serve in small petit-four paper cups on a cut glass dish topped with a sprig of holly leaves.

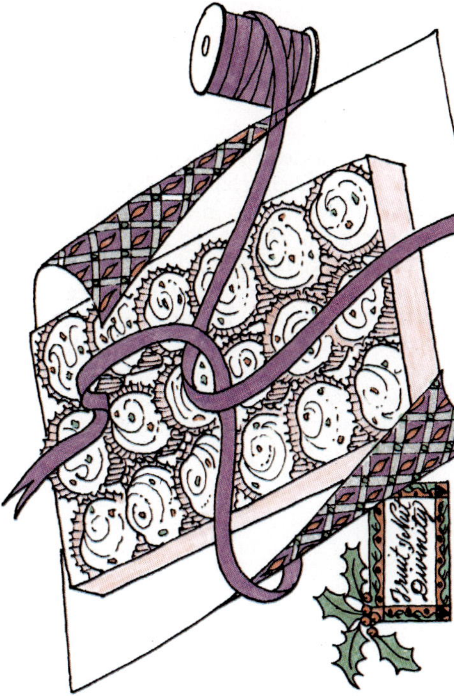
Fruit & Nut Divinity

3 cups sugar
1 cup light corn syrup
1 cup water
3 egg whites, beaten stiff
1 teaspoon vanilla
½ cup chopped nuts
¾ cup candied fruit

In a 2-quart saucepan combine sugar, corn syrup, and water. Cook, stirring, until sugar dissolves. Then cook to hard-ball stage (260°F). Pour syrup in a thin stream into beaten egg whites, beating at medium speed until mixture begins to thicken. Add vanilla, candied fruit, and nuts. Then beat with wooden spoon, lifting high to incorporate air until candy is very stiff. Pour into buttered square pan to cool. Cut into squares. Let dry until firm and wrap individually in waxed paper or store in a tightly covered tin.

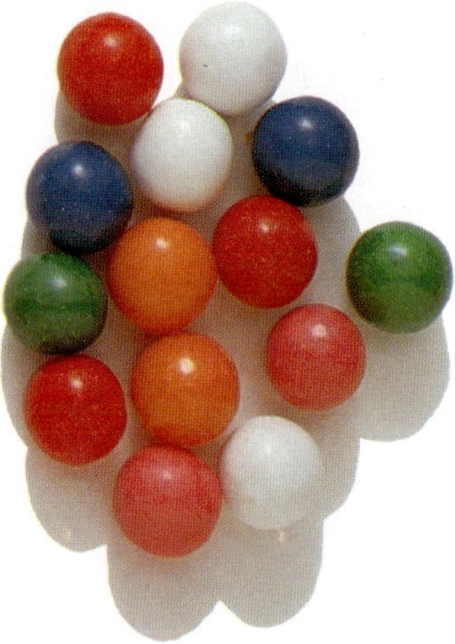

Candied Nuts

- 1 egg white
- ½ cup sugar
- 1 teaspoon salt
- ½ pound (2 cups) pecan or walnut meats
- ⅔ cup butter

Preheat oven to 300°F. Beat egg white until very stiff; add sugar and salt. Fold in nuts. Melt butter in shallow baking dish or pie plate; add nut mixture and bake 30 minutes, stirring several times. Remove nuts from oven and spread on brown paper to dry. Store in airtight container.

Holiday Rum Balls

   3 cups crushed vanilla wafers
   1 cup confectioners sugar
   2 tablespoons cocoa
   3 tablespoons corn syrup
   6 tablespoon rum
   1 cup finely chopped nuts
       Confectioners sugar

In a bowl, mix vanilla wafers, 1 cup confectioners sugar, and cocoa. Add corn syrup, rum, and nuts. Mix together. If necessary add a few drops of water so mixture holds together. Pinch off small amounts of mixture and roll into balls. Roll in confectioners sugar. Let stand 60 minutes, and roll in sugar a second time. Store in covered container for 2 or 3 days before serving. Makes 3- to 4-dozen rum balls.

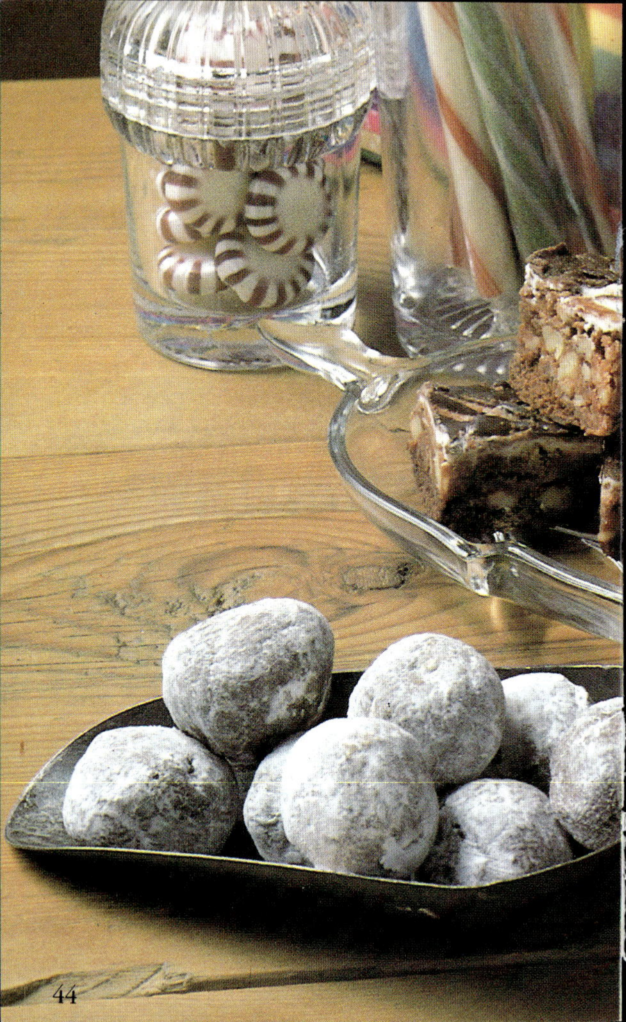

45

Chocolate-Mint Sticks

1 batch "Chocolate-Nut Squares" batter
½ teaspoon peppermint flavoring
½ cup chopped almonds or walnuts
2 tablespoon butter or margarine
1 tablespoon heavy cream
1 cup sifted confectioners sugar
1 tablespoon peppermint flavoring
1 square unsweetened chocolate
1 tablespoon butter

To the batter for "Chocolate-Nut Squares," add ½ teaspoon peppermint flavoring and chopped nuts. Bake at 350°F for 25 minutes in a 9 x 9-inch baking pan. Let cool on rack. Cream together 2 tablespoons butter or margarine, cream, confectioners sugar, and 1 tablespoon peppermint flavoring for frosting. Spread on cake. Let the frosting harden. Melt together chocolate and 1 tablespoon butter. Spread on top of peppermint frosting. Chill and cut into oblongs.

47

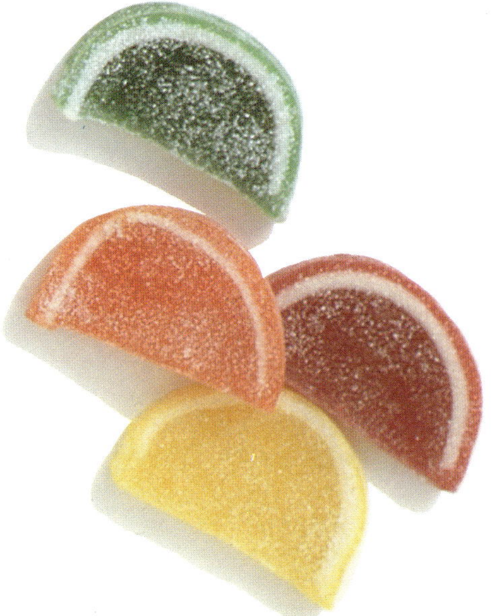

Candied Fruit Peel

1 grapefruit peel or 2 orange peels
Water
Sugar

Candied Fruit Peel is a delightful garnish to use on cakes, pies, puddings, etc. It is also a refreshing candy after a meal.

Remove white pith from rinds and cut peel into thin strips about ¼-inch wide. Place in saucepan and cover with cold water. Bring to boiling point, drain, and repeat process three times.

Dissolve ½ cup sugar in ½ cup water; add peel and boil until all syrup has been absorbed. Cool, roll in granulated sugar, and spread to dry.

Gift Idea:

Wrap candy—firecracker-fashion—in yellow cellophane and tie both ends with lime-colored ribbon. For a truly elegant wrapping use a salvaged pale blue Tiffany box (or your local best). Line the box with foil and pile in the candied peel. A small, white fork might be placed in with the peel.

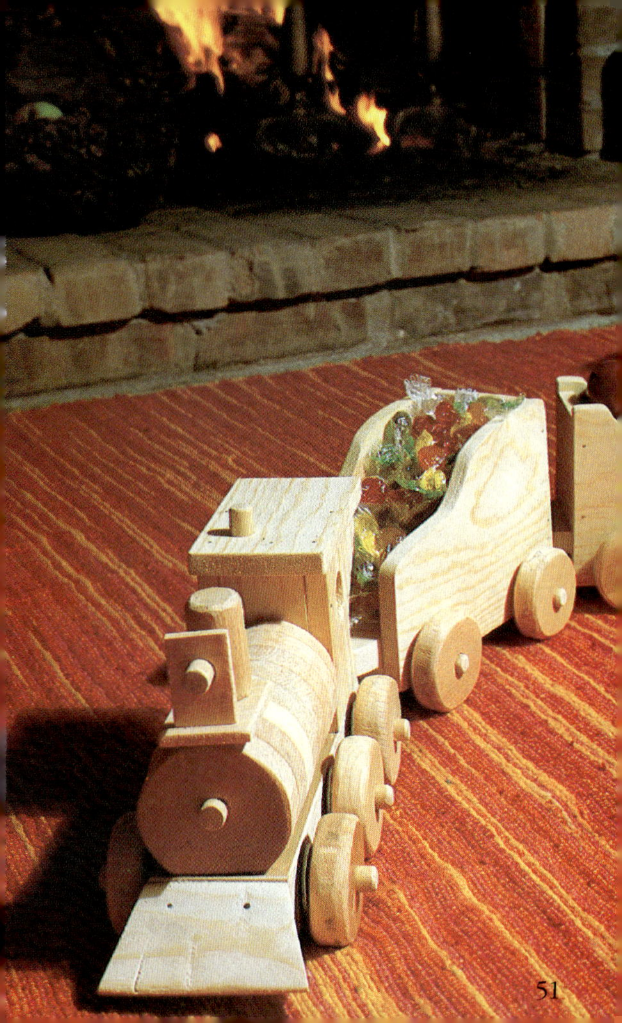

Candy/Cookie Brittle

    1 cup margarine
    1 teaspoon salt
 1½ teaspoons vanilla
    1 cup sugar
    2 cups flour
 1½ cups semisweet chocolate pieces
  ½ cup finely chopped nuts—macadamia, pecan, walnut, etc.

Preheat oven to 350°F. Blend together margarine, salt, and vanilla. Beat in sugar using an electric mixer at medium speed. Stir in flour and chocolate pieces. Spread dough evenly in ungreased 10 x 15-inch pan. Sprinkle with nuts. Bake 20 minutes. Turn onto wire rack to cool and break into irregular pieces. Store lightly covered.

Gift Idea:

Wash out tomato or other vegetable cans and cover with gift wrap. Stack brittle in clean cans. Seal cans with foil or plastic film, and tie with bright gift ribbon.

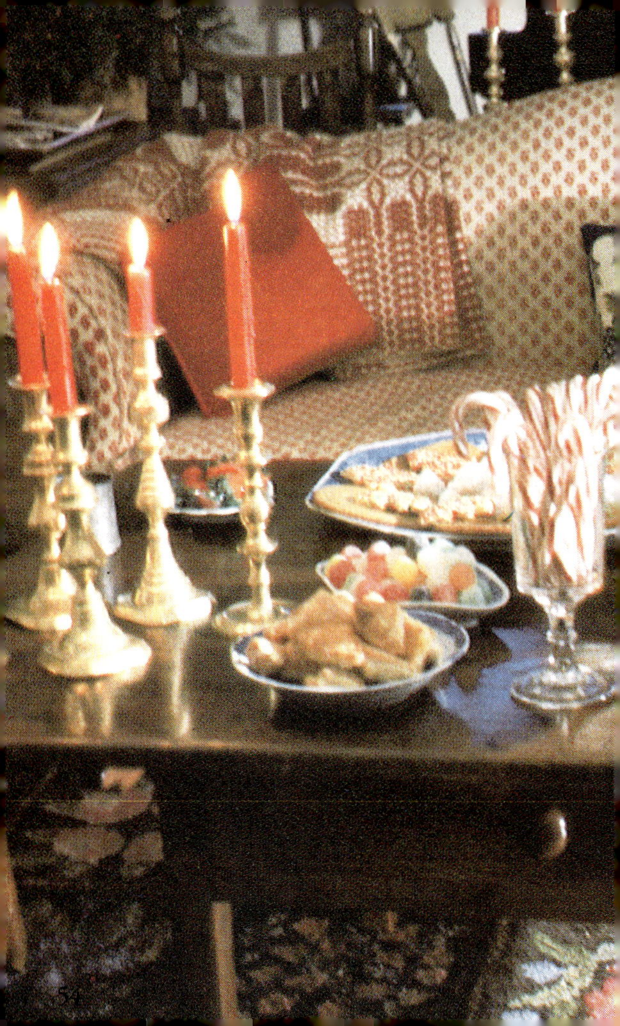

55

Chocolate-dipped Fruits

- 2 cups semisweet chocolate pieces
- 1 tablespoons vegetable oil
  Toothpicks
- 4 cups whole strawberries, large maraschino cherries, dried whole apricots, etc.

Melt chocolate pieces and oil in top of double boiler over hot, not boiling, water until completely melted. Using toothpicks dip fruit half-way into chocolate and allow to cool on waxed paper.

These candies are the priciest things at New York's posh chocolate shops. Serve on stemmed crystal plates or in individual foil candy cups. Or add these to a dried fruit and nut platter, include a cocktail fork, and wrap in plastic film for a special gift to your host or hostess.

Cream Caramels

    4 cups sugar
 1½ cups light corn syrup
    6 cups heavy cream
    1 teaspoon vanilla
      Vegetable oil

Gift Idea:

For gifts, save little boxes throughout the year (square, oval, round, etc.) and cover them using doll house wallpaper or small patterned gift wrap. A small saucer picked up at a tag sale also makes a pretty container for these rich little confections. Arrange the caramels one layer deep on the saucer and overwrap them with plastic film. Or wrap it in waxed paper and glue on a paper doily for a pretty topper.

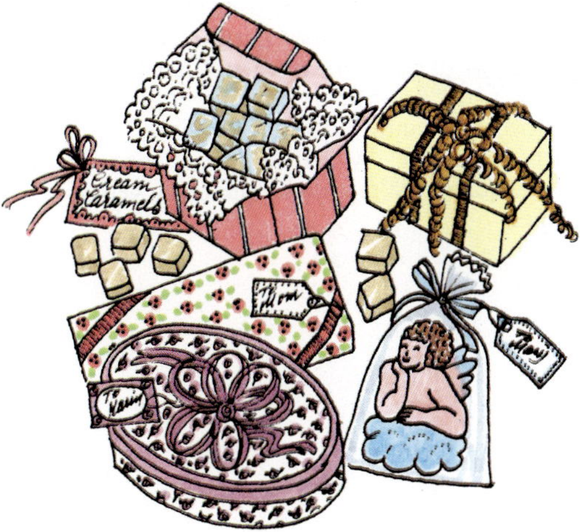
Cream
Caramels

In a 3-quart heavy saucepan combine sugar, corn syrup, and 2 cups of cream. Stir constantly until soft-ball stage (240°F). Slowly add 2 more cups of cream and cook, stirring, until temperature reaches 240°F again. Add last 2 cups of cream and cook until mixture reaches hard-crack stage (300°F). Stir in vanilla and pour immediately into large oiled pan ¾ to 1 inch in depth. When cold, cut into 1-inch squares. Wrap each square in waxed paper.

61

COLD-WATER

The cold-water test can be used to
is not as reliable as a thermometer. Re
test. Spoon out one-half teaspoon of sy
Note behavior of syrup and refer to c

Stage	Temperature
Soft ball	234°–240°F
Firm ball	244°–248°F
Hard ball	250°–265°F
Soft crack	270°–290°F
Hard crack	300°–310°F

EST

...ge stages of the candy syrup, although it
...ve the pan of syrup from the heat for each
... and drop into a glass of very cold water.
... below.

Behavior	Examples
Syrup forms a soft ball that flattens on removal from water.	Cream caramels Penuche
Syrup forms a firm ball that holds its shape.	Caramels
Syrup forms a hard ball that holds its shape but is still pliable.	Divinity
Syrup separates into threads that are hard but not brittle.	Taffy
Syrup separates into threads that are hard and brittle.	Rainbow Crystals Poppy Seed Candies

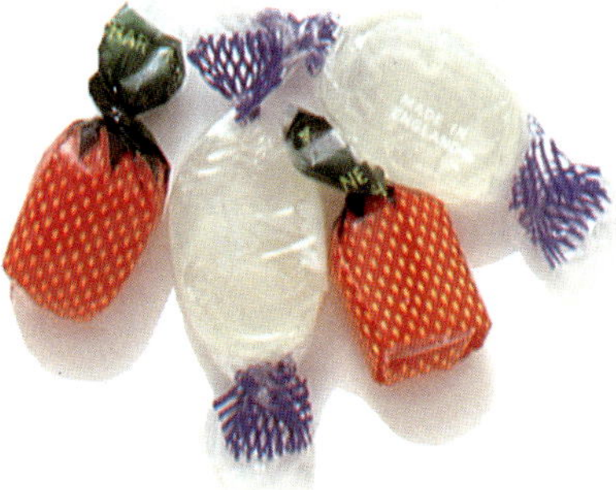

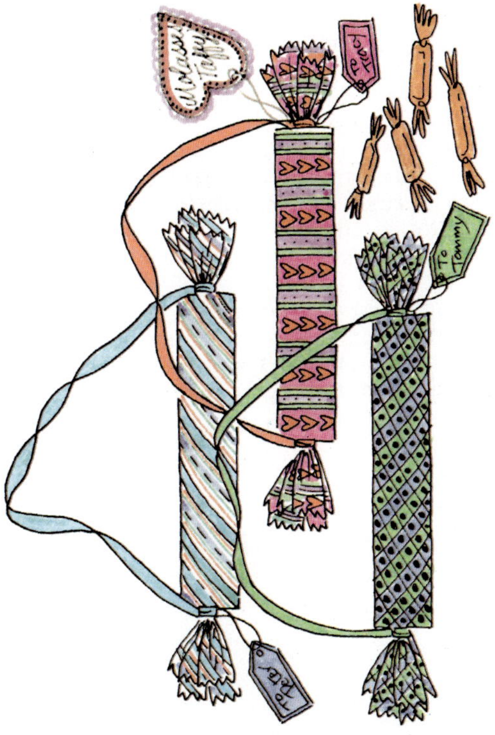

25

This candy is best made with a friend or two, to help with the pulling.

In 2-quart saucepan cook sugars, molasses, and water together, stirring only until sugars are dissolved. Boil uncovered without stirring until syrup reaches soft-crack stage (270°F). Remove from heat; add vinegar, baking soda, salt, and 3 drops oil flavoring (if desired). Stir only until all ingredients are incorporated, then pour onto a large buttered platter. Allow to cool for 10 minutes or until candy can be handled but is still warm. With buttered fingers pinch off about ¼ of candy and pull and twist until firm and light, forming a 1-inch rope-like strand. Using buttered scissors, cut off pieces and wrap each in waxed paper twisting ends to seal. Store in covered containers.